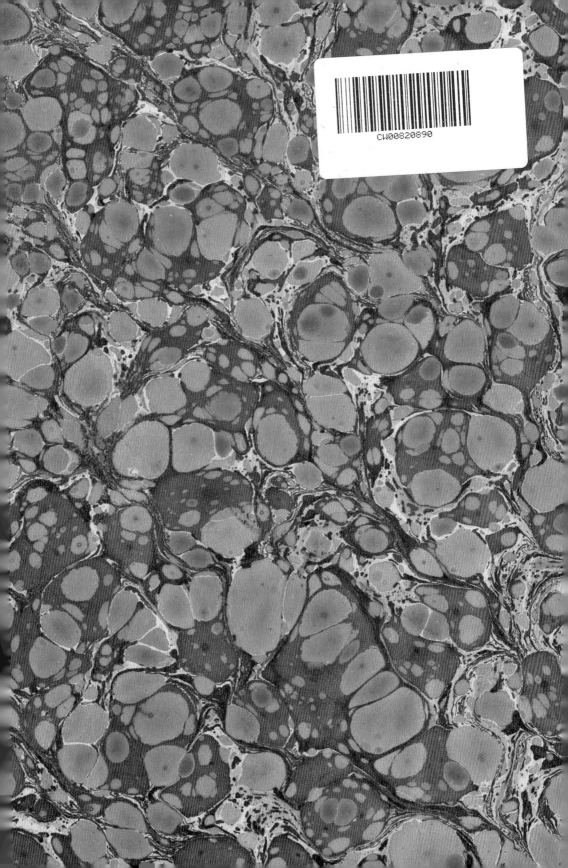

THE TIDE'S MAGNIFICENCE

THE SONGS & POEMS
OF
MOLLY DRAKE

CONTENTS

Kashmir August 42

THE TIDE'S MAGNIFICENCE
by Gabrielle Drake

My mother was always something of an enigma – starting with the year of her birth. She was born in November, in Yangon, capital of the ancient kingdom of Myanmar – then under British rule and known, rather less romantically, as Rangoon in Burma. But the year of her birth was always shrouded in mystery. She belonged to that generation that considered it discourteous to ask a woman her age. So, if anyone was so impolite as to inquire, she considered it perfectly legitimate to tell a white lie. Thus, till the day she died, I believed she was born in 1916: only when we came to inscribe her tombstone did her beloved sister say "we cannot lie before God" – and the correct date was carved, which was 1915. It was, after all, a very small white lie.

In preparing my small part in this book I have been led again to read her diaries: only a few are extant – though I suppose the miracle is that there are any at all, given the extent of geographical turmoil in her early life. They are immediate and vibrant, and conjure up the Molly that most people would have met – a delightfully engaging

7

and warmly loving person, for whom 'fun' and 'happiness' seemed to be vital ingredients of life. There is little trace of the Molly who could write the poem *Two Worlds* or the song *Set Me Free*. The darker side of Molly was known only to those closest to her. This was mostly due to her fierce guarding of her private self; but it was also because she was brought up to believe in the old British adage "mustn't grumble".

The diaries begin in 1929, when Molly was thirteen years old — though the first entry (made on August 29th — no diary starts on January 1st) has the tantalizing phrase "read old diaries". Were they hers? Or someone else's - the inspiration for her to start writing her own? The schoolgirl diaries are typical documents of their era, revealing a more juvenile, though perhaps more literate, teenager than her modern counterpart. They show exuberant love and loyalty to all those closest to her: her two sisters, her parents — sorely missed but never forgotten in their enforced absences in Burma — and her beloved Aunt Helen and Uncle Willie: the couple who became second parents whilst her own were far away. Although she professed to hating school, she seems to have been a good and interested student in all subjects except the dreaded mathematics. How she struggled with Arithmetic, Geometry and Algebra! None of them made any sense to her, and her wailings in her diary are heartfelt and poignant for anyone with a similar problem.

But above all, Molly never seems to have been bored. Pleasures may have been simpler and more restricted than those on offer today, but she reveled in them, and one can see the beginnings of her delight in nature in the walks that were an inherent part of leisure activity. Not that walking could have been listed amongst Molly's favourite activities, certainly not in her adult life. She wrote just before beginning her grueling war-time trek out of Burma into India: "These feet were not constructed for walking".

Fri: 18th

Woke up. Got up. Had breakfast. Walked by town to
school. Form meeting prayers.
Algebra. Ugh! I really am
very stupid at maths I suppose but ★ algebra is like
a foreign language to me, and
I do hate Mary Roberts she
always turns & laughs when I say
something silly, which I suppose
is quite natural, but......
Drill with Tucker. Break. Two periods
of drawing. Yum! Yum! Lunch.
Practise in yellow dorm. Practised
lace half time, & then played in
a game. Had a bath. Tea. English
with Bull dog Drummond. Prep.
Supper, & Reading. Have finished my
Embroidery.

Sat 19th

Woke up. Got up. Had
breakfast. Oh! I've forgotten
to put that yesterday I
got my cloak. Lovely! Nice
bright orange hood, & so warm.
Form meeting & prayers. Maths,
Latin, Break, Rems, prep &
a P.L. with the Tom. She
will persist in calling me Mary.
Lunch. Practised a little. There
was a match up Marlow, First school
v Seniors. Wycombe present, beat
Seniors hollow. Cicily ripped
the knee right out of her stocking
& looked so funny. She shot all
the goals after half time. I
do think lacra is a pretty
game. Had tea. Played screaming
charades in Parlor. Came back. Barry
did their performance. Jolly good.

Sadly, there is a large gap between the diary that documents her first sea voyage to Burma after leaving school in 1933 (maddeningly it ends the day the family sail into Rangoon's harbor) and 1939, when, at the beginning of World War II she and her husband Rodney made an extraordinary journey to the USA by boat — a business trip for him. Sailing into New York harbour obviously inspired her poem *New York*.

The most intriguing diary is perhaps the one that documents her enforced flight, with her sister Nancy, from Burma to India to escape the Japanese invasion of Burma in 1942. Her account of the (mostly) organized march vividly brings to life the exhausting journey that evacuees were forced to make: it is curiously intimate: practical, lyrical, amusing, observant — and uncomplaining. It is so very much a Molly document.

Fear and uncertainty were understandably constant factors:

"...it was all rather fun at first if you could manage to forget why it was that we are all here anyway. I find I can numb my brain into not thinking how really awful the situation is, with Rodney down in Rangoon and the raids getting worse every day and goodness knows how they'll all get out if Rangoon falls..."

"...I wish to God I knew if Rodney was still in Rangoon. Oh lor how I do hope he's gone with the rest of the staff to Mandalay but I'm terrified he's either been left behind to blow up the mill or been pinched by the army... The situation doesn't seem a bit good. I should think Rangoon will go — how incredible to think of our house and all our possessions in enemy hands — our *little* house, oh dear..."

"...Rangoon has fallen - oh hell and damnation. I got a surge of awful sick dread about everything when I was in bed. I always notice I get most frightened and worried when I'm lying down..."

Tues: Oct. 17th.

We were called at five thirty
& staggered out of bed to
watch the sun rise out of
a very grey mist. It didn't
stay out long & everything
was very grey & dim. We
had breakfast & said good-
bye to our steward & then
went up on deck & watched
as we moved off towards
New York. We stood on the
top deck & as we leaned
over suddenly out of the
mist rose a dream city
with grey towers & spires,
and then the sun broke
through and very very faintly touched the tops of
the buildings with a

suspicion of gold. It was
the most beautiful sight
I've ever seen. After that
we had to dash from side
to side of the boat so as
not to miss anything.
On the other side was the Statue
of Liberty which is vast &
very impressive. Then New
York came closer & the sun
gradually changed the city
of mist into the city of
bricks & mortar & steel and we
sailed up the river & finally
came to rest in one of the
docks. We didn't get off
the ship till about 4.30
what with passports etc.
to cope with. Then we
had to wait ages on

"... The moon was just coming up behind the trees on the cliffs — beautiful and full, the beastly thing. I never thought I would come to hate the moon as I now do knowing that it will mean an interrupted night for my love and an almost certain visit from the little yellow bastards... Didn't get to sleep for simply ages, the moonlight was so lovely on the quiet misty river. God damn it...."

But these entries are rare, and mostly she succeeded in keeping fear at bay

"...Were woken with tea at 6.45. It was still quite dark. We had an awful scramble trying to wash and dress and do our faces in this tiny tent. Then we had breakfast by a fire. The sun had just risen and it was fresh and cold and you couldn't help feeling happy and full of well-being. Really almost anywhere is beautiful in the early morning, and the jungle is lovely — so dewy and nice-smelling, and a very very blue sky..."

And "numbing my brain" did not involve numbing her powers of observation: her diary is a lively record of everything and everyone that surrounded her, from her fellow travellers:

"...she's rather the born-to-sorrow-but-bearing-it-patiently type — a bit Madonna-ish and could look very nice if she tried, but has 'put away her mirror for the trip' — a pity..."

to the countryside she was walking through:

"... We started off in pitch dark, and climbed up the paths out of the cleft where the camp was ... and got to a path that went along a sort of knife-edge of hill with valleys falling away miles below on either side. It got light gradually and we could see far down into these valleys where, every now and then grew foamy-looking trees of white flowers which looked just like cherry blossom. Later we found one growing near the road and it was Bauhinia, which has a lovely white waxy flower rather like an orchid. ... at about half past seven,

12

some lovely music playing, and sat in the heart of the Burmese jungle and heard Big Ben strike in Parliament Square! I shall never not think it simply wonderful. June Nancy & I got terribly giggly doing our hair at bedtime & June told us such a silly story about her headmistress at school. I had to get out and go a'wandering in the middle of the night and it was all blotched moonlight & shade & very still except an occasional crack made by an elephant in the distance breaking a branch & the clock-clock of

the wooden "kalawks" they wear round their necks. They are turned loose at night & feed themselves, and in the morning each "oosy" can always find his own elephant, goodness knows how.

Saturday Feb 28th
Four miles today to a camp called Yeson which was rather like the last - a shady patch of cleared jungle near the same stream as yesterday, but further into the jungle. I went & watched Gwyn Bailey, facing Anthon, Thorshes so that I could do it another day. Lunch came round with the mail and there was

we got to camp at about 12.0, a rather filthy site at a place called Dah Thway Chauk site. Red & Joanne had gone on with the elephants & said they found it simply disgusting with clouds of flies from the first party's leavings. It was a clearing in the jungle but a very hot place with hardly any shade. We sat for lunch in the middle in full sun. It was terribly hot and sweaty in the afternoon, but it rained a little & was then a shade cooler. June was more or less laid out after Friday's march & they are going to have the stretcher for her from now on. I don't! I found a tick in my hair & had to pull it out.

how how they thought she could do all these marches without tiring, & here is she's 3½ months gone already, & poor thing it is horrid for her.

March 2nd Monday
Waited in the jungle while the elephants were loaded, and nearly died of cold. A nice short march, only 3½ miles almost all in shade. At 10.30 crossed a wide shallow stream - the elephants had already been turned loose into it - and then we were in the camp - a nice shady site. Nancy had a bit of a fracas at lunch with Red & Jeanie

13

we rounded a hill and suddenly came upon the most wonderful view I've ever seen in my life.… It really looked like the promised land stretched out below us, hills and valleys and spurs away and away to what looked like the sea in the distance but was really the plains. And all in the amber and coral and blue-green of very early morning. An entire country laid out before us like a child's plasticine map."

And comments on the living conditions along the route:

"Our cabins had no bunks so it's Mother Earth again for us tonight. We went in search of some water to wash in and discovered the total water supply for this camp consists of one tiny muddy puddle. The lavatories were most extraordinary. Huge holes in the ground like young caves with a very rickety branch placed across them on which you had to balance. You perched on the branch and were in constant danger of plunging head-first into the abyss below. Oh for a lovely white seat with a plug to hand and a very firm lock on the door!"

The final part of the journey was undertaken by bus — but this seems to have been even more arduous than the walk:

"...There were no seats in the bus and no springs either and no surface other than dust on the road... And of course there was no glass in the windows so that cloud after cloud of thick yellow dust swirled in and covered every mortal part of you. Talk about "And their mouths were filled with dust" — so were their eyes, ears, noses and hair — also their teeth.

But in spite of everything, and being jolted and bumped till you felt sick as a cat and the back of your neck ached, Nancy, Jonah and I had a lot of fun and lots of silly jokes....I can't tell you what Nancy and I looked like, our faces were dark brown with white owl-like eye-holes where our glare glasses had been, and our hair — what there was of it that was not tied up — was as grey as a woman of sixty's..."

And when the two sisters finally reached Calcutta:

"...N and I had our first long bath in a thousand years. Oh the joys of civilization! As I let myself down into the water, an unmistakable brown flea detached itself and struck out for the shore..."

The first civilised Breakfast.
M.D.   Nancy.

A page later, the account ends.

So we do not hear about the last leg of the journey from Calcutta to Delhi, where Molly and Nancy were given shelter by their uncle and aunt, Alan and Mary Lloyd. But we do know that Alan and Mary became deeply loved members of Molly's family, and that their house, 5 Cavalry Lines, was the inspiration for at least one of her poems (*Full Moon*). Mary, who might have been a formidable memsahib, but who championed the weak and vulnerable, (she founded the Delhi branch of The Society For The Prevention of Cruelty to Animals - surely no easy task in India at that time) was the subject of Molly's poem *For Mary*.

We also know that this period of refuge was prolific for Molly, and that many of her poems were written in Delhi. None appear to have been inspired by the redoubtable journey she had just made, and few by her quotidian surroundings (with the possible exception of *Lost Blue*). In this time of turmoil and crisis, she turned to worlds that must have seemed lost forever. Did she find comfort in the memories that produced *London* and *New York*? Gain security from poems about the English countryside, such as *Cock Lane*?

Perhaps the most revealing poem of this period — the one that in many ways illuminates the paradoxes that were inherently Molly — is *The Ambitious Moth*: an epic tale of a little moth whose ambition to 'reach for the moon' is both understood, lauded, but ultimately doomed. Ambition was not unknown to Molly — but it was fairly low down on her list of priorities. I think she realized, but somewhat deprecated this in herself.

It certainly led her to undervalue herself. Which is perhaps why her songs and poems have for so long lain hidden. For I don't believe that, given the choice, she would have wanted them to remain so. Whilst their creation was a private and internal journey, I think she thought of them as children: once born, they had their own independent lives to live. Certainly there is evidence to suggest that, in the early days, she showed her poems to a few influential people. And I can vouch for the fact that, many years after my brother's death, she was pleased when the then head of Island Publishing asked to hear her songs.

But as she herself wrote in *Warning to Heroes:*

"He cannot, who is well content at heart
Ride out the stars undaunted and alone"

As far as her everyday self was concerned, Molly Drake was surely well content at heart. She deeply loved her husband and her children, and creating a home for them became her primary purpose in life. I never had the feeling that she was champing at the bit of independence. But then again, I never had the feeling that we consumed her entire spirit. There was always a part of my mother

that remained unknowable, unattainable and her own. All of us —
especially my father — understood this. It was no mystery to us.

The philosopher Peter Russell defines the difference between
'mystery' and 'mysticism' thus:
" 'mystery' is a lack of knowledge frequently resulting from the
silence of others, 'mysticism' is a fullness of knowledge brought
about by personally retiring from the world into a state of inner
silence."
Molly was familiar with this state of inner silence. *The Shock of Dying* is
a poem written as a direct result of an experience she described in a
letter to her mother:

"... only a few days before I had been trying to describe to someone
the very strange feeling — revelation almost — that I had had on that
night journey in India — which had prompted me to write the poem.
The extraordinary feeling of suddenly being much *wider* - of being
incorporated with things around, and of having slipped through
the ordinary bounds of consciousness and personality. I know it was
a most wonderful feeling and I seemed to have found for a moment
the answer and solution to both living and dying. I can't describe it
at all and nor does the poem — I suppose the sensation didn't last
long enough to catch hold of it properly..."

Was it this understanding of a wider consciousness that enabled her
to face with such fortitude the ultimate tragedy of her life - the death
of her son Nick? Indeed, after all the years of being nourished and
protected by her husband Rodney's love was it now she who gave
him strength? Certainly they drew comfort from each other — and
gave comfort to young strangers who would turn up unannounced
on their doorstep in search of the source of Nick's magic. Not that
Molly would ever tell them about its one obvious ingredient — her
own music and poetry. It would never have occurred to her to do so.
She never thought of herself as anything other than 'an amateur'.

Much of her work is more profound than she ever gave it credit for. It is also wry and self deprecating — and above all, brief. If I had to choose one poem that for me showed all these qualities, it would be *Martha,* which opens:

"I sometimes think when it is time to die
I may perhaps have learned the way to live…"

And ends

"…And so I go stumbling and all perplexed,
Puffed on the dreary wind of little fears,
An eddied leaf jostled upon the tide
And seeing not the tide's magnificence."

I suppose we always underestimate our parents. It is probably a necessary part of growing up. I loved and admired my beautiful mother. But only now do I fully realise how clearly she saw the tide's magnificence.

(Below) Molly with sister Nancy to her right

Molly as DJ on All-India Radio

With Rodney in fancy dress

With Gabrielle

... and with Nick on a shopping spree

Sailing on The Trent, July 1936

MOLLY DRAKE
The Poems

To me a poem is not a
for-ever thing — nor the
statement of long-held
views — but the product of
a moment so suddenly &
hurtingly felt that it has
to burst out into words.
The happy & enduring things
do not evoke or provoke
poetry —

Martha

I sometimes think when it is time to die
I may perhaps have learnt the way to live,
I may have learnt to sift from out the grain
The chaff of littleness that blurs my eyes,
Small worries, little thoughts and little ways,
That creeping canker of insignificance
That eats away the very heart of life
And leaves behind the dull and flaccid shell.
I live hard, and oh, I hardly live
If living is become life's only business.
And so I go stumbling and all perplexed,
Puffed on the dreary wind of little fears,
An eddied leaf jostled upon the tide
And seeing not the tide's magnificence.

Jhelum, March 1944.

Will O' The Wisp

Deep in the caverns of the inner man
There lives a nurseling: mischief-minded elf,
Begat and born in truth of man's own self,
And trouble-maker since the world began;
A wild and wicked urchin none can tame,
For on the decent murkiness of sight
He flicks the golden pollen of delight,
Imagination is his prosy name.
And he may beckon you with glancing steps
In jewelled sandals, winking like a star,
Into the oozy marshes, till you are
Floundered and lost amid their sucking depths.
But following this wayward lead men come
To those wide halls the poet knows for home.

The Sloth

O day, you come so silently
Stealing upon me as I sleep
And burst unheeded through the night
Apollo's early tryst to keep
Your fiery fingers chide the sky
Bidding her furl and hide away
The alien banners of the night
And swear allegiance to the day,
And burnished splinters prick the gloom
With dazzling shafts that set to flight
From shadowed corners where they lie
The lurking minions of the night.
But in my bed I turn again
Hunching my shoulders sleepily
And screw my eyes against the glare
And curse the day for waking me!

The Tall Trees

The rooks are awake in the tall trees:
For many and many a year
They were the voice of the tall trees;
Now in the dusk we hear
A cawing, as though they would break their throats
On a jagged cry of sorrow,
Taking their leave of the tall trees
That are coming down to-morrow.

The Pinewood

Out of the hot white sunlight into the pinewood,
Suddenly into the deep and resinous cool
Meeting hands and eyes with the shock of plunging
Into a midnight pool.

From the most arid blinding of the senses -
Imagination burnt away with sight -
Comes back the haven of renewed awareness
Waking in slow delight.

To lie on this gentle earth where the bedded needles
Have carpeted the years a friendly brown,
To breathe again the shadow-speckled forest,
Is knowing the way to drown,

To drown within the fullness of gathered waters,
Where sleep and silence and all of death began,
Finding the peace that lies at the core of a whirlpool,
The still small voice that speaks in the heart of man.

Kashmir, September, 1944.

Full Moon

The deep enfolding silence, pricked out with tiny sounds,
Stretches hands in benison and passes on its rounds,
And passing sets each waiting thing within its healing mould:
The drifting snow of alyssum, like snow to touch and cold;
The bull-frog in the lily pool with golden lidded eye;
The moon-drained stars, like water drops, clear in the pallid sky;
The shadow of the bended rose creeping the misty turf -
The shadow dark, the rose itself paler than ocean surf.

Up where the dappled mulberry leaves their secret places keep,
Pressed safe and close against the bark, a lizard dares to sleep;
But in the stone-arched doorway where deeper shadows lie,
A little waiting rabbit sits with ever open eye,
He never sleeps, nor ever stirs, but keeps his watch alone
For this is the ice-pale kingdom of he whose heart is stone.
And lying white beneath the moon, and girt with friendly trees
The quiet house is fast asleep, lost in its memories.

5 Cavalry Lines, Delhi, 1943.

After Rain

The sigh that stirs in the trees when rain has ceased
Of lingering raindrops dripped from leaf to leaf.
The darkness is a warm expectant gloom,
Waiting and still and filled with mystery
The rainwashed smell of earth and growing grass
The musty smell of sodden twig and branch...
A murmur moves throughout the shadowed depths
Blown by a tiny wind that heralds dawn,
And unseen from a thousand leafy hides
The crickets twang their sharp metallic note
An endless pattern of unchanging sound
Whose sameness is a silence in itself.

The Ambitious Moth

To you, who beat your bodies in the night
In frenzy on the uncurtained window-pane,
Recoiling but to best yourselves again
In the abiding struggle after light;
And who, when summer nights are warm and damp,
In bickering halos round the drawing-room lamp,
With every sign of festival debauching
Practise the wilder joys of wing-tip scorching:

Who, keener than an arrow to its mark,
Come hurtling from a deep and dusky lair
In quiet hedgerows, into the blind glare
Of headlights jabbing through the country dark;
To you I sing, out of the years' dim vista,
A song of one who is a long-dead sister,
And if a mothy tear or two may glisten
No harm in that: stay then your wings, and listen.

She was a milky silky little moth,
Her body white as hoar-frost on the lawn,
Her eyes the opal skyline of the dawn,
Her wings were finely woven damask cloth,
And spotless as the under-wing of doves
Her white silk stockings and her white kid gloves,
Pouting and soft her small and furry breast,
And she was lovely - lovely but distressed.

For when the sun has dripped his liquid way
With fussy pageantry beyond the world,
And wanton cloudlets frisk, all dipped and curled
With running fire, hirelings of the Day,
To make his going seem more consequential;
And when, with hands folded and reverential,
Twilight appears, and bats begin to ply,
And only pool and puddle hold the sky,

Then kindles in each mothy soul a spark,
And wing-tips quiver as the fever burns,
And every lepidopterous eyelid turns
Towards the lanterns prickling in the dark.
Then hasten they to where, with glistening tears,
The lofty tapers drip the chandeliers;
Or storm, against the power of the will,
The crofter's candle blinking on the hill;

Or find a beacon flaring in the gloam
Waking the tousled fields to ruddy morn;
Or batter on the swinging pane of horn
And fret the weary shepherd, bound for home:
All, each and every one, with wings astir
Obey the summons, saving only her
Of whom we sing - she could not follow after,
And to be different does not make for laughter.

And so did sadness guide her through the year,
For never had she felt the surging tide
Leap up to sweep her diffidence aside
And bring her strength and warming; alien were
These clammy fires, and alien through and through
Her body felt, and single strangeness knew:
The knowledge in her breast was like a knife
Slashing to open emptiness her life;

And she was lonely as a shell new-wetted
And thrown upon a white unpitying shore,
Thrown from the cloisters of the ocean floor,
The twilight green with coral arches fretted;
From safety of the broad and bosomed sea
To stabbing daylight: even thus was she,
Knowing the pale seclusion of her heart,
And so was lonely - lonely and apart.

One day, in summer time, it came to pass
At evening, when the fickle light was waning,
She watched her brothers, sisters, cousins straining
To be away; and hidden in the grass
She closed her eyes in weariness a space,
And when again did open them, the face
Of all her little world had known a change,
Was wild and luminous and wholly strange.

She cast about with fear and sense of doom;
Then was her heart with mortal anguish wrung,
For in the sky a mighty lantern hung,
Whose piercing glory stripped the night of gloom
And flung the doors of Heaven open wide;
The stars were pale with wonder by its side,
And all the universe was held in awe
And silence at the miracle she saw.

She gazed and gazed, and, trembling, sought to borrow
The strength to bear this phosphorescent dawn,
Her lungs were empty and her body torn
With joy that has no life distinct from sorrow.
The meaning of the world was in this second,
And she must follow where the glory beckoned,
So with her senses pulsing to a swoon
She cried and sprang towards the risen moon.

Before the full, one day as yet remained:
The zenith known but only half possessed
Still holds a measure of the tingling zest
And flavour sharpened in the unattained.
The moon, in lordly splendour of his prime,
Had yet to make the last triumphant climb,
And knew, within this brief and brittle hour,
The high wide exaltation that is power.

And power she felt throughout her body streaming
Uplifting her, and not a pang nor falter
Profaned her journey to the great high altar.
The air was colder now and heavy-seeming,
A jealous night stood guardian in the sky
Her shining blade of purpose to defy,
And with a cruel curling scorn he pressed
His bitter lips against her stiffening breast.

The world became a vast tormented throbbing,
The pains of all the earth were in her wings,
Yet as the swan, near unto dying, sings
She sang; nor heard her singing change to sobbing.
Joy leapt in her with every wounded breath,
Laughter and hope, and love that mocks at death.
And so she perished in that far-off night
Her frozen eyes turned upward to the light.

Well, there's the tale and it may serve to use
As caution unto her who strives to wander
Past earthy confines, seeking what's beyond her,
(For this is doubtless wrong - but you shall choose.)
Or if you wish it take this lengthy talk
For those who aim to fly before they walk.
But Mother Moth, knowing the story, tries
To council truant offspring in this wise:

"My daughter, do not spread your wings too soon,
Remember now, no flying for the moon!"

Delhi 1943

The Collector

Butterfly-thought with golden daggered wings,
How shall I net you? There's the unending riddle:
Quick now, I have you - next a drop from the bottle
And there! But I like you not with
   a pin through your middle.

Song Of The Flute

The water lies cold in the shallow pool.
Still and cold and filled with withered leaves,
Drifted and blown across the sandy edge
To lie, forgotten, in the silent pool.
And silent through the soft and chilly air
Creeps in the sadness of the fading year,
The flat and quiet sadness of ended things,
That makes a numbness deep and small in the heart.
A little listless wind with mournful breath
Sighs in the reeds – the pale and brittle reeds
That, yesterday, so green in the sunlit air,
Tomorrow will be rimed with early frost.

Delhi November 1942

Waning Moon

So lies the world, deserted pale and cold,
Under the dead grey ashes of the forsaken moon
Wandering lost in the empty crypt of the sky.
Here is the squeezed and shrunken rind of the moon,
Her sickened light breathing of all decay,
And lingering on like an uninvited guest
To mock the lean and haunted shape of the dawn,
That slinks like a hungry cat between the roofs,
To scratch the pickings from the sad grey walls,
And turns, unsatisfied, away.

Jhelum, December 1943.

45

The Wind

In those wide grass lands where the wind is hurrying,
The shadows race with the white clouds' scurrying
Flown with the reckless wind where the bended grass
Shakes in the yellow sunlight as the shadows pass.
Under the open sky clean-swept and free
The beech clumps twist and sigh with
   the noise of the sea...
And since the beginnings of this ancient earth
In the groping darkness of that struggling birth
The wind, from the mighty cavern of that icy dawn
Sweeps down the ages on and on and on.

When warm red brick and cold grey steel
Tower and spire, thatch and eave,
When the last cog and crank and wheel
Crumble and rust beyond reprieve,
When age-old stone, cathedral-grey,
Turns with the slowness of decay
To rubble, dust and chalky clay
Then in the stillness of breaking day
In the first pale light from the hollow sky,
The wind will rustle and murmur and sigh,
Shiver a little, be out and away
And those freed lands, their burden gone,
Will turn their heads to the rising sun,
And blessed with lightness - newly grassed,
Will joyfully bend as the wind rides past.

Rangoon, December 1941.

The Thaw

Brown and blue and heather blur,
Dazzling sky-pools shaking
Among the mud-ruts: creep and stir
And sounds of thrust and breaking
Unheard beneath a hedge of song.
A sleep so dark and dead and long
Is worth it for this waking.

The Clear Rejoicing Water
I

The clear rejoicing water comes leaping down
Over the pebbles, river-smooth and brown,
Laughing and wild over the stony track,
Downward, onward, never looking back,
Splintered with sunlight - shaken with noisy mirth,
Caring for nothing and no one on this earth;
Mocking the dripping ferns that grow and must be still,
Moving unfettered, and of its own free will.
Water is young and clean and good and cold
   as a two-edged knife,
Water is everlasting - water is life.

The Clear Rejoicing Water
II

The water, a little wearied, borne on the summer tide,
Has reached a place of quietude wherein to hide
And rest a little, lost in the cool
Untroubled heart of a secret woodland pool,
Guarded and green with over-leaning boughs,
Where shimmering dragon-flies, unmoving, drowse,
And twisted roots dip down as the brown earth shelves,
Where wood anemones lean out to watch themselves
And drop their thread-veined petals one by one
Into the shallows dappled in shade and sun,
Rocked, as the widening ripple stirs and sighs.
Water, compassionate and wise,
Is like an ended pain, and drawing quiet breath,
Water is everlasting, water is life - and death.

Delhi, May 1943.

For Mary

Call in the shy and shaggy-coated ponies
Whinnying lost in the drab and dying light,
Call in the scattered sheep from the empty hillside
And let them be warm at my fire tonight.

Call in the tired tender-breasted pigeon
Beating her trusting wings in the bitter height,
Call in the cold, the patient, the inarticulate,
And let them be warm at my fire tonight

June 30th 1944

The Valley

The birds come wheeling out over the valley
Quivering in the hot still air on steady wing,
Gliding, turning, hovering unmoving,
And on the sun-warmed rock their shadows fling,
Shadows that curl and stretch like grey cats waking
Drowsy in the sun and no sound making,
The valley is filled with sun and lonely silence.

The birds come wheeling out over the valley
Their shadows big and dark on the yellow stone,
Down in the valley it is very quiet
And in the stillness the shadows move alone,
And faintly murmuring comes the drone of flies.
The sunlight in its eternal bright aloofness
 Is a fat and smiling god with cruel eyes
Unheeding all this little earth's despair.
What sleeps in the valley with the sun and silence?
Only the wheeling vultures know or care.

Early Blossom

A little drift of yet unmelted snow
Beyond the hour of thaw: a little foam
Torn from the skirmish of the angry sea
And caught upon the melancholy boughs,
The same that did not shirk the bitter season
Nor bend before the scourge of wind and weather;
That with the gathered dignity of years
Stood out the ancient nights affrayed with stars
Grown bright to madness in the thorn of frost:
The same that now are graced before their time,
Since from the woody entrails is reborn
The chilling sweetness of this early bloom,
More white than white before a sullen sky,
More pure than purity, and stark of scent,
Unless it be the taste of running water
Fallen in rocky shadow till the noon,
And stinging cold under a thirsty mouth.

O strong and wise, and lovelier for the doom
Whose darkness whets the riven edge of light,
Do you not feel the menace in the air
Lurking along the chicken-run and crept
About the stiff and barren orchard grass
Unkindled yet by that green fire-maker?
The world is old, mourning and alien,
But you are come to play the harbinger,
To fling a challenge under winter's gaze
And cry the promised reawakening.
But in the clear wild crying is foregone
For ever your appointed destiny -
The steady garnering of warmth and light
And consummation in the broadened sun.
For you, the quenching and oblivion,
The long unbroken sleep in the quiet earth
And nothingness: only the pointed flame
Burning within the shrine of ecstasy.

Jhelum, December 1944.

Cock Lane

I walked in a country lane at dusk,
All in the soft and foggy air,
In a secret twilight cold and hushed
Alone I was walking there.

I smelled the smell of turned brown earth
Lying in fields beyond the hedge,
Quiet fields that are drained of light,
Waiting content for the touch of night
At the steep wold's edge.
Along the hedge, a pearly smoke,
With every pale and tufted plume,
The traveller's joy has spread its cloak
Like foam spilt in the gloom.
A fretted oak with mossy bark
Leans out to me, remotely near,
Wrapped all in mist and shadow-dark.
There are no frightening spaces here,
The fog makes all things close and kind;

Dripping brambles that I could find
Heavy with sodden winey berries;
Humble haws, as red as cherries,
Little and gay in clustered herds
The best-beloved of hungry birds;
And filled with honey-golden pips
Flaming thorn-encircled hips;
And bryony tendrils binding me
Here in the lane eternally.

For somewhere deep in the hedgerows wet,
Where the lane looks up and bends to the hill,
And twilight greets the approaching night,
Alone, I am walking still.

Delhi, May 1943.

The Crow

I never thought that I should know
A moment when the homely crow
With gaping beak and strut absurd
Would seem a lovely-plumaged bird;
Nor dreamed I could be grateful for
That harsh and inharmonious caw,
Yet when the shadow falls across our days
Who knows to what the spirit leans in praise?

Nineteen Thirty Nine

And he came
Walking over the rough ground,
His feet, where the skin is stretched to the bone,
Were stained with an unhealed wound.
And the people braced themselves to meet him
Sullen, muttering, armed with stones,
Till nearing them with weariness he spoke:-
"The day of each one ends
So keep your stones my friends
You will need them for each other
Man for man - brother for brother,
Why waste your stones on one
Whose day is done?"
And he went from them walking alone
Limping a little on wounded feet
Nor did they see him more
In the cloud of approaching dust.

Rangoon, October 1940.

1940

I see the fertile fields of France, the golden grain,
The vine bowed down, the creaking market wain,
The rich, brown earth that richer harvest yields.....
The hand of darkness is on all these fields,
A shadow moves throughout this lovely place,
The body sacrificed for this fair face,
For this bright countenance the throbbing flesh
Is racked and fettered by the steely mesh,
And while the face no branding-iron warps
The living body is become - a corpse.

Rangoon, September 1940

Rodney Drake, Simla 1942

August 28th 1944

But yet the dead may rise again,
And as the smoke of battle blows
From the dark earth, a tongue of flame
Is fanned to life and warmer glows:
And they who let their citadel
Crumble, break and fall apart
Hold it again with lifted heads
And quickening of hand and heart,
And standing square with opened eyes
Know that in this, redemption lies.

Warning To Heroes

And when the bays too easy grasped appear,
And when the nagging fever bids you rest,
And when at last you cease to find most dear
The bright and glittering image of the Quest,

Beware, beware - for then the tide is spent
That brought you to the summit of the mountain,
The onward road lies only in descent -
A quenching of the spirit's icy fountain.

For satisfaction proves a poison dart
That undermines the laurel-girded throne:
He cannot, who is well content at heart,
Ride out the stars undaunted and alone.

A Prayer for Love

If I must love at all why then.

        in sooth

Let me love truly - but let me

        love the truth:

Let me love clearly & know what

        I'm about

Not build a waxen doll & pull

        pins out,

Or think behind some certain

        brow & eye

My own creation must in duty

        lie.

Nor weep for death of what I

        planned to find.

Give me a love that is in no

        part blind

That into two open eyes can

Plainly
~~clearly~~ see

Up & down & through - & yet still

        be:

If I've a prayer for love let it

        be this: —

That I love wisely, well & love

        what is -

A Prayer For Love

If I must love at all why then in sooth
Let me love truly - but let me love the truth.
Let me love clearly and know what I'm about,
Not build a waxen doll and pull pins out,
Or think behind some certain brow and eye
My own creation must in duty lie,
Nor weep for dearth of what I planned to find.
Give me a love that is in no part blind -
That with two open eyes can plainly see
Up and down and through - and yet still be:
If I've a prayer for love, let it be this:-
That I love wisely, well, and love what is.

Colder Than The Dew Drenched Stone

Colder than dew drenched stone,
Silent, unmoving and alone,
With nothingness in your blind eyes,
In icy chastity your body lies
That once did warmly bend to mine
And twist me backward, and with arms entwine
My very heart whose leaping beat
Made death itself seem sweet.
And if we then had died
Should we be lying coldly side by side?
No - we should fly in the rushing breath of night
Or shiver in a meteor's piercing light
Eddying upward to a star-pricked sky.....
Why then without me did you have to die?

Olean, N.Y., October 1939.

Escape Me Never

Then I will go, be out and about and running
The last and longest race of the stricken leaf
Driven upon the breath of the lees of summer,
- And as I go I shall outstrip my grief.

Outstrip it, shake it, leave it far below me,
And turn my face in the wild sunlight above,
Go like a flame and leave it lagging and weary,
Limping along with the cripple that was my love.

Go where the white cloud-cumulus is churning,
Go where the tortured wind flowers gasp and bend,
Go till I reach where the road has no more turning
- And there's my grief to meet me at the other end.

Murree, October 1945

The Prison

Man has created time: and always striving
To burst the barriers of his own creating,
He draws them tighter with the weight of living,
And clangs the padlocks with a load of hating.

Yet when he loves, with startled eyes espying
That chink in the prison wall that closes never,
His poor heart cries, and full believes its crying,
"World without end - for ever and for ever."

Murree, September 1945

And When I Look At You...

And when I look at you my heart is still,

Still as a waiting bird alert with fear,

And numb and deep and quiet in my breast

A flame of thought is saying: You are here.

Then drowsily my blood begins to flow,

The warmth of sleep comes creeping in my veins,

And weak and heavy does my body grow,

Shot with the throb of tiny, piercing pains....

But I can only sit, too still to sigh,

And follow with my eyes as you pass by.

Rangoon, May 1940.

Cry Of A Very Young Girl

You cannot tell me it is not a wonderful thing
To be utterly lost in another human being,
So that ordinary bones and hands and hair and eyes
- The mortal load so endlessly in tow -
Take as their garment all the glorying
And splendour of night skies
And are not flesh:
And yet are very so.

My Love

My love, your heart is like a rolling drum,
Your eyes are looking out across the world,
I cannot see, I dare not, but I know
How your whole soul lies in them unawares.
So silent, yet silence filled with our twin thoughts
Beating about like captive birds in pain
Imprisoned in the cage of our despair.
Lift up my head - the time has come to take
My last look in your eyes and I shall see
Myself reflected there, my dwelling place.
This is the moment guarded out of Time
Within whose boundaries lies all my life,
Oh my dear friend beyond it there is none
No future and no living any more.

London, January 1936.

Bacchus

O Bacchus, why do they always have you
Pot-paunched and flabby as a jelly
With tangled whiskers; a bulgy blear-eyed sot?
No Bacchus - I will shave you
Give you a leopard's grace.
Your red-brown eyes are hot
With wine and love and laughing,
Great laughter, welling from a lean smooth-sinewed belly
To the bare throat: and your bronze temples hung
With grapes and vine leaves.
You of all people shall be young.

Love And Beauty

This is the law that all men know
Love is for Beauty: this being so
Love in its casket waits for those
That flower in beauty like the rose.

This is the law all women know
Love is for Beauty: this too is so,
But beauty has a broader span.
This is the law then, this is true
That should she love a one-eyed man
All one-eyed men are beautiful too.

Well, It Is Finished

Well, it is finished -
And we who trod the skies in joy and dread,
Have reached the time when we must travel back
To the admittedly more easy track
That other mortals tread;
The gods, you see, can't be for ever treating.
(Lie still my heart, I will not have you beating.)

Yes, it is finished,
And that fantastically be-jewelled season,
Each moment spangled with its own sharp lustre,
Has flattened out and cannot quite pass muster
In the drab light of reason.
The pudding's proof, my dear, is in the eating;
(Or would be, if my heart would stop its beating.)

And, being finished,
How wise to know, and even find it pleasant
That deep within the eye, the winking prism
Is but a healthy glint of cynicism,
And not a tear, unshed, but ever present;
We both have known such things are only fleeting,
(Then what's the use, my heart, of all this beating?)

We know it's finished,
And we have said "Of course we'll still be friends",
And when we meet, with friendliness I take
Your hand and hold it, just for old time's sake,
This is the way that all such poignance ends -
This gentle uncommitted hollow greeting
(But for my heart and its eternal beating.)

The cup we drained will be anew replenished,
I shall not even turn to hear your name,
Oh yes, my dear, how finally it's finished!
And this old heart keeps beating just the same...

Delhi, February 1943.

Epitaph

The candles flutter in the stone-damp air,
Clumsy with fallen wax and short and bent,
The candles gutter and the candles flare,
Their little brilliant life is nearly spent,
And in the gloom, a smoky wisp, they die...
Here in the tomb the children lovers lie,
And men have wept for them throughout the years,
For men don't weep the same sweet-bitter tears
For love grown old and tired and decayed,
For lips that wrinkle and for eyes that fade,
For hearts striving to sing that are not blithe,
For all the sorrow spilled by Time's long scythe.
And so these two for tragedy are famed,
Who in the hour when the dark stranger claimed,
Were wrapped within the bright and aching fire
Of youth's own loveliness of warm and sweet desire,
And close in life, their love without regret,
In death, forever young, are closer yet.

Delhi, August 1943

Nasim Bagh

The faint, dull sheen of water, still as the sky,
At whose edge blurs and drifts a thin, white mist,
Dark mirror of the night and dark encircling hills,
Their black and ragged battlements aslant
A shallow bank of pale, star-tinted cloud.
The straight-stemmed lotus buds are grey with night,
Unwinking drops quicksilver the flat, grey leaves ;
And green frogs chirp from tangled beds of reed,
Chirp, and are silent, watching with star-touched eyes
Where the black ghost shadows of those other hills
Lie sleeping in the secret heart of the lake.

M. D.

Molly's only-ever published poem found in an Indian newspaper written for the British emigres

Nasim Bagh

The faint dull sheen of water, still as the sky,
At whose edge blurs and drifts a thin white mist:
Dark mirror of the night and dark encircling hills,
Their black and ragged battlements aslant
A shallow bank of pale, star-tinted cloud.
The straight-stemmed lotus buds are grey with night
Unwinking drops quicksilver the flat, grey leaves,
And green frogs chirp from tangled beds of reed,
Chirp, and are silent, watching, with star-touched eyes,
The black-ghost shadows of those other hills
Sleeping in the secret heart of the lake.

Kashmir September 1942

Iver

How quiet flows the river here at Iver,
The rushes are all bended under water
Like drowned hair, loose and outward streaming
Beyond the torrent and beyond the pain.
Oh that the river flowed in me so stilly
Leaving the tumult of the foaming weir-head,
And like the reeds bent all my bones with quiet –
Then I could lay me down a little while and sleep.

A Place Revisited

A place revisited is a sorry thing,
Dusty, flat and savourless, the same
And yet so different from that other place
That lay asleep within the wanderer's heart,
Bright with the secret fire of memory.
Here is the empty shell of what you loved,
Stripped of the garment that you wrapped it in
The thing you gave it that is now forgot
It lies, forlorn, under an empty sky.

And when again you trespass on this ground
And thus discover all its nakedness
Then you have robbed your inner sanctuary,
For what you loved & guarded through the years
Is utterly destroyed, forever lost,
Vanished to nothing, as the long-shuttered tomb
Crumbles to dust with the intruding light and air....
And you are left this bare, unlovely thing
To carry with you throughout all your days.

Simla, October 1942.

Dog On The Wheel

It doesn't matter where you are
From John o' Groats to Zanzibar,
Nor how you go nor what you do...
You think "Oh, deserts in Peru
If I were there and knew that clime
I should be free." But all the time
Unalterably along the route
Yourself is chained to either foot.

The Travellers

We, who were all so full of warmth and laughter,
And loved each other well - and said good-night,
Come warily into the morning light;
The spell of sleep has clad us all in sable,
And we have been so far, we meet as strangers
At the breakfast table.

New York

The dawn is sulky and the mist is grey,
Shrouding the waking of an early autumn day,
On the smoky water the drifting sea birds cry,
And the steady homing ship is grey as the muffled sky.

And then the waiting heart is still, holding a chill of fear,
For something that is not of this earth is slowly drawing near,
And stealthily, from out the mist, there grows before the eyes,
The phantom of a citadel, whose dreaming towers rise
Like sentinels of silence, and brooding vigil keep
Over a city lost in Time - a city made of sleep;
A city stolen from the mist, unrooted in the ground,
Her summit breathed in saffron light - a city halo-crowned,
That man might seek two thousand years and never, never find,
But having seen, what should I care if my two eyes were blind?
For I should have this miracle, undimmed by further sight
Forever in the nothingness of my eternal night;
For here is timeless beauty, having not age nor youth,
Beauty for man's unresting heart, beauty that is not truth.

For as I gaze, the haunted light has broadened, and the sun
Is up and to its earthly task - the towers one by one
Are gold and bold and glorious and great and straight and clean,
But that which lived before is gone, and might have never been,
And in its place, a town of light, and in my heart a sigh...
But look to where the spires climb against the dawning sky
Look up at them my cheated heart, look up at them and say:
"The dream is past, the dream is dead -
    but this is a new-born day!"

Delhi, July 1943.

London

What is there left to say about London?
Bound in mist and forever free,
And the river that flows through the heart of London
Out to the Northern sea....
The river that flows with the pulse of London,
Old and brown and flecked with oil,
Rolling down from the sweet Thames Valley
Over the English soil.
And the gentle, incessant rain of London,
That often falls from dawn to dark,
Till the rueful sparrows fluff their feathers
Drenched, in the London park.
The bitter winds blow from the East in London,
And whip the river to brownish foam,
And the summer, hot-tar smell of London
Welcomes the wanderer home.

Delhi, February 1943.

Evening In The City

All day it has been raining in the town
In sooty runnels down the chimney stacks,
Leaping, gushing, dancing on the leads;
And like a row of shiny hat-pin heads,
A minuet in duns and greys and blacks,
Fleets of umbrellas went bobbing up and down.
But not towards the very end of the day:
The rain is done. The city sheds its load,
And there's a little peace in all the faces.
The sky has laid itself right down in the road,
So we go walking in exalted places.

And I can see the grass, shining and wet,
Pushing undaunted through the pavement stones,
The traffic grinds unendingly, and yet
High in the elm-tree tops the night wind moans
A secret and complaining faery wail
Full clear and sweet above the swish of cars.
And all the bryony blooms are ghostly pale
Climbing the hedge towards the early stars.

The Road To Mandalay

Silent and still the jungle stands
Rigid with heat in the noonday glare,
Comes the creaking, carping shriek of a bird
Through the bursting air....
Nothing that I have ever seen
Is better than what I am seeing now,
Red-brown earth and startling green
And the feathery grey of a dying bough,
The blue-green haze of wooded hills,
Bauhinia bowed with snowy freight
And the hush of noon
Disturbed alone
By the purr of the Buick Eight.

And my eyeballs ache
And my skin's on fire
And I've got the thirst of twenty-five,
But for all the beer
In this hemisphere
I wouldn't have missed this drive.

Kalaw - Thazi, April 1937

The Journey

What does it feel like setting out unfriended?
Pushing off from the bright familiar land
And crossing where the fringe of twilight foaming
Laps the whiter sand -

For then the grey gloamed sea is waiting for us,
The cold wave trembles making gentle moan,
And looking back, the land is almost hidden,
And we are alone.

What does it feel like – can nobody answer?
Many have journeyed on that lonely swell
But no-one, having crossed the wide pale ocean,
Comes back to tell.

Midnight Mass, Penn Church

And now the organ's softened note
Shivers, and eddying up and up
The shadowed rafters, dusty, dim,
Whisper and sigh the dying sound.
The polished brass in wall and tile
Emblem of long forgotten men
Gleams mistily with borrowed light
Gives back, diffused, the amber glow
From crowns of candle flame.
The swinging incense dips and bows
The blue smoke twists in spiral coils
Sweet, cloying, spicy, pungent smoke
That with the smell of dusty cloth
Of leather, worn, and rubbed with time
Binding the musky sheaves of prayer,
Of polished wood and winter flowers,
And burning, molten tallow wax,
Mingles to fill the drowsy warmth.

Outside, the still, keen breath of night
The waiting tombstones, moisture-cold,
The ringing earth - the ringing bell
That echoes on frost-sharpened air
To bless the sleeping fields.

Rangoon, November 1938.

The Ruin

There is a shaft of sunlight thin and cold
Creeps down from the upper window; in it the motes
Move listlessly like little vacant souls
Lost in the brightness and knowing not how to go:
And all the quiet of the old forsaken church
Is filled with echoes of the deepening years.

Under the sagging rafters of the roof
Murmurs the long-imprisoned organ note,
Captive within the hollow courts of Time;
Or is it only the keening of the wind
That lifts the trailing cobwebs and bestirs
The brown mouse-velvet bat that flutters down
Like a leaf in autumn, and spreading sudden wings
Swoops and is vanished in the chancel glooms?

The ivy has spread her green inquisitive fingers
Over the pulpit and twining there holds fast;
The withered grasses take their seats to pray
Amid the crumbling pews, and drift on drift
The dead leaves rustle gently down the aisle.

Jhelum, January 1944.

The Ruin.

There is a shaft of sunlight thin &
                                      cold
Creeps down from the upper window; in it
                              the motes
Move listlessly like little vacant souls
Lost in the brightness & knowing not how
                                          to go.
And all the quiet of the
~~He lonely here in the~~ old forsaken
    is filled with   church,
~~And whispers the~~ echoes of the deepening years.
~~filled with the whisperings of forgotten~~
                    ~~days.~~

Under the sagging rafters of the roof
                  long-imprisoned
Murmurs the ~~captive echo of the~~ organ
          pulsed & quivering in the wings of time
Or is it only the keening of the wind
That lifts the dusty cobwebs & bestirs
The brown mouse-velvet bat that flutters
                                    down
Like a leaf in autumn, & spreading suckled
                                     wings
Swoops. & is vanished. in the chancel glooms.
~~swooping is vanished in the shadows.~~
The ivy has spread her green, insensitive

fingers
              twining
Over the pulpit & ~~twining~~ there holds
                                    fast,
The
~~The~~ withered grasses take their seats
                              to pray
amid
~~Among~~ the crumbling pews, & drift on
                                     drift
The dead leaves nestle gently down
                        the aisle.

After

From the great high pinnacle of After
I watch the world go round
And hear the mad ones' laughter
And the dream-boats so aground.

Aground on the stones of the floor of the world
Where the shadows crawl about,
But how can they prate on the floor of the world
When the bottom has fallen out?

After

From the great high pinnacle of After
I watch the world go round
And hear the mad ones' laughter
And the dream- boats go aground

Aground on the stones of the floor of the world
Where the shadows crawl about,
But how can they grate on the floor of the world
When the bottom has fallen out?

The Bench In The Park

The old man's asleep on the bench
Where this morning the children played:
Boots, cracked and shabby, turning out,
Hands in, palms up, cuffs frayed;
Shoulders dragged and sagged and heavy
With all of weariness,
And mouth that tells too much without
Its day-time guardedness.
A little drab, a little lost, unlovely and forlorn
Here sits and waits his work-day shell, like clothes unworn

Or house untenanted. For where is he? Not here;
Not here, but in that other wide dominion,
Unconquered in the broad and boundless place,
Riding upon a taut out-quivering pinion
Down through the long cool rushing glades of space.
Not here behind those wrinkled lids, those fingers
curled and slack.
Don't shake him: for it is a grief to watch him struggle back.

1945

Lost Blue

In the deep uncertainty of the night
The blue plate hangs on the wall,
And I wonder - is it really blue at all
Or was that stolen by the thieving light?
And who can say whether it will return?
Oh how the quiet plate must yearn
For her lost blueness in the dark,
For though the day has brought it oft before,
She cannot quite be sure.

And how can I be sure in the uncertainty of the night,
That dawn will bring the same world back again?
I take for granted the ceiling will be white,
And shadows long, and the yellow morning light
Limpid with a little midnight rain,
And apples lying rosy where long grass grows,
But no one really knows.

Delhi, June 1943.

The Killers

My nurseling child,
With feet like birds and eyes that are wild,
How shall I save you from their hands?
Wrap you close in swaddling bands?
Keep and hold you in my breast
Safe and warm to take your rest?
When all the time through the wall I hear
Voices that mutter, lips that sneer
And spit on their weapons, bright for the crime,
"Something to do dear - to kill the time."

Primary Colour

My son is three, so his views
Are not over mellow;
I gave him a violet to smell
And he said it smelt yellow.

"Smells sweet, you mean" I said:
The intractable fellow
Replied that it didn't smell sweet
It smelt yellow.

The Mind Of Memory
Three Sonnets
I

The mind of memory is a land we know,
Where we most happily may walk about,
Because we know exactly how to go,
And which the paths that best are sorted out
And left untrodden: we know the stony ground
Where ways are ominous and quagmires deep.
We make a sudden detour where we found
The stream too wide, or precipice too steep.
And that long grinding hillside, set with thorns,
Where shame went with us even to the crest,
We bypass – for our wiser journeying scorns
The places where we were not at our best.
And so through many comfortable hours,
We tread the pathways that are trim with flowers.

The Mind Of Memory
Three Sonnets
II

The mind of memory is a dusty book,

Fetched from the highest of the library shelves,

And opening at random we may look

At verse and chapter written by ourselves.

The pen was ours', the printer's ink was Time,

The publishers are Destiny and Fate;

And not a syllable of prose or rhyme

Is lost, nor colour faded from the plate.

The thoughts and happenings of yesteryear

Drowned since many a time in dumb forgetting

Are suddenly presented sharp and clear

As in the instant of their bright begetting.

But who would look on them must firstly gauge

The secret that unlocks each folded page

*There is no 3rd Sonnet. Or at least, our searching up till now has not revealed it.
Was it ever written?*
*It is interesting – but probably fruitless – to speculate as to what it might have
said, but do the last two lines of sonnet 2 contain a clue?*
*Molly being Molly, the chances are that Sonnet 3 would have been a darker
exploration of the recesses of the mind.*

Lost Grief

As we were walking down the street,
There came from a high up open window,
Six notes of music: then her feet –
As though the road were suddenly steep
And heavy with a summer's heat –
Came slower, and very slow.

"Stop and tell me why you weep,
Turn this way and look at me –
Does it remind you of a time
When you were sad?"

"Ah no,
But it reminds me of a time
When I could be."

On Waking

Have you not thought sometimes on your returning
How alien earth's features seem to be?
How there is not one single lantern burning
To light the way across the deeper sea
That separates the known from the unknown?
(The known in this case being whence we came
The unknown the dark shadow-peopled earth:)
Torn then we are from the immaculate flame
Into this region of a narrow birth,
Where there's no element to our true breathing fitted,
Where all is governed by unaccustomed laws,
Where the serene of light is freaked and pitted
And speckled with innumerable flaws;
And where the unencumbered spirit, knowing
The vasty ranges of a timeless going,
Jars, and is sickened with unfamiliar dread
To find itself chained, bodied - and in bed.

Dawn

The pebbles whiten in the dawn
Where darkness lately trod
And from the sleeping rim of earth
Rides out the lord of all rebirth
A god-head and a god,
And light from night is born.

The sheep that nibble in the mist
Lift up their woolly heads,
And far across the valley gaze
To where the slumber-folded haze
Is tattered into shreds
Of trailing amethyst.

The tingling air a promise gives
And midnight grief is stilled
Because all things are new again
Redeemed with night-begotten rain
A promise unfulfilled?
Maybe – but now it lives

Murree July 1944

The Intelligentsia

Who was it set the poor blind shuffled words
To make fools of themselves, hobbled nose to nose?
For up and down the wide and formless road
More dismal sounds the clanking of their chains
Than from the much-detested prison yard
Whose name is Meaning.

Jhelum, April 1945

I Have Gone Stale

I have gone stale;
And words that were their own illumination
Are guttered candles, and the acrid reek
Of greasy wax upon the senseless air.
There is no length nor breadth nor resonance,
No fluted arch of many-patterned sound,
Only the muffled clack of wood on wood.
Passion is worn away, and sentiment
The scabby crust that rims fomented jam;
Tears are no tears but drops of glycerine
That flow and flow, but oh, how stickily!
The phrases of our usage, words and thoughts,
That pulp away throughout a myriad mind,
Are wrung and used and utterly despoiled,
No virtue left in them nor sustenance.
Then how should I, born thus unfairly late,
Turning aside the too familiar dust,
And kicking in the rubble of the years,
Come stub a toe against a new idea?

But though I am as stagnant as the weeds
Upon a meadow pond close-hung with trees,
Where black and gassy bubbles wink and pop,
Yet that bedizened strumpet men call Nature,
With the insensate prodigality
That bursts the ripened foetus from its bonds
Even into an over-teeming world,
Must have a hand in purging out of me
What's there begotten. So the mill must turn -
I grind me out my feathered poppy-cock,
And little comfort in reflection find.
There's not a man across the senile world
Who needs must read what I am forced to write.

Jhelum, December 1944.

Remember This

Remember this when you are full of woe:
There never was a grief time could not mend,
So often do we think of time as a foe,
We do forget that time can be a friend

Tears

There are tears for the word - the lovely word
Like woven banners flying:
Fool I may be but I seldom have heard
Poetry read without crying.

There are tears for another, not often shed,
And wholly good as I see,
Scarcely leaving the eyelids red,
Purging a tautness free.

But the deepest, ugliest, saltest tears
Are the tears that I cry for me.

Cut Out The Corn

Cut out the corn,
The aching pest,
The curving thorn
That bites the breast,
That long has torn
And long oppressed,
Cut out the corn.

But when it's done
Don't turn and scorn
Your rest.

There Was No Glimmer

There was no glimmer left of what had been;
My heart was like a gourd, ripe with its pain,
And bitter-tasting to my longing tongue.
I looked in vain to find the haggard sun,
But all the time the day blew to its end,
A gusty shapeless day full of grey wind,
Whose music was the loose door hinges moan,
The curl and scrape of leaves on the pavement stone,
And the blind massive plodding of human weight
Towards the uncertain comfort of the night.

Murree, September 1945.

This Moment

You talk of the beauty of the moment: well, I would hate
To decry that. But you see there are no glass cases;
Nothing remains inviolate;
And the more of light and beauty to-day, the more
    of sorrow
Lies within this moment,
For to-morrow.

The Rift

In the flat organised surface
Of the solid unbroken plain,
Stretching smugly to the horizon,
Accepting wind and rain
And summer's glare and winter's bleak exposure
Without a wrinkle in her sleek composure,
Silent and orderly under a yawning sky,
Comes a tiny crack, widening like a woman's cry,
Widening until those deep foundations shake,
Menacing as a dark destructive snake,
Splitting the proud indifferent land asunder,
Gathering force until a crash of thunder
Lays bare the core within the panting earth,
The gaping wound of a crude gigantic birth.....
For this undoubted shame
There is a name
And it is Mirth.

Dalhousie, August 1943.

Cold Nose

Cold nose
A faithful friend,
Cold wind
Summer's end,
Cold hands
Warm heart,
Cold bed
Lovers apart,
Cold steel
Fallen hero,
Cold blood
Fiddling Nero,
Cold shoulder
Cutting stare,
Cold feet
Dentist's chair,
Cold comfort
Wealth - one day,
Cold meat
Monday.

Simla, October 1942.

April Things

No more the blackbird sings...
And yet these thoughts of April things
These dreamings and such kind,
That should have been left far behind
With old forgotten Springs
(When reason, dozing in the wings
Was dumb and deaf and blind)
Do leave in the dry grass of the mind
Unfading faery rings.

The Two Worlds

There are two worlds: one is flat
And filled with light and dust and common living
And the trust of day following day;
And here we say: "He died,
Hadn't you heard - it was so sad,"
But nothing can really touch us, good or bad,
We go our way, riding upon the swell
And all is well.

But the other world is round:
Arched like the roof of a dark cave,
Full of the sound of beating wings and water dripping.
And to whisper here "He died"
Is the streak of wings unseen on the cheek,
The creeping widening roundness that perfectly fits
The hollows behind the ribs: the water drips,
Thin, emasculating, under knees and spine,
With the long low curdling whine of the beast at the door.

This is the world of the hours of three and four
When life goes down bare-foot on the rippled sand,
Down with the slacking tide to the furthest ebb,
And only a strand, thin as a spider's web
Holds us above the final broadening crack.
The strand recoils to drag us back
To the flat pale sunshine; but if the little thread,
Worn upon jagged rock-edge, be destroyed,
Then for the streeling plunge to the sick void,
Down through the splintered dark, down and down
Through the arching universe, the perfect sphere,
The absolute ultimate roundness of the shape of fear.

Jhelum, March 1945.

The Shell

Living grows round us like a skin
To shut away the outer desolation,
For if we clearly marked the furthest deep
We should be dead long years before the grave.
But turning about within the homely shell
Of worry, discontent and narrow joy
We grow and flourish, and seldom see
The outside dark that would confound our eyes.

Some break the shell. I think that there are those
Who push their fingers through the brittle walls
And tear a hole: and from this cruel slit
Stare out across the cinders of the world
With naked eyes: they look both out and in,
Knowing themselves and too much else beside.

The Gulf

Then ultimately only I am I
An entity more lonely than a star
Treading an orbit separate and far
In regions of my own perpetual night:
And oh, there is no comfort in these lands,
No borrowing of any other light
Only a stretching of most groping hands
For who's to hear a cry
Across the encircling gulf?
Another planet – out of another sky?

Beauty Is Gone

Beauty is gone:
And yet the hand that took it left the job
Half-done. And through the deepening dusk
Goes pulsing on
The time-uncaring, unrepentant throb
Within the husk.

June 1951

Spring Flowers

If in the Spring I die you must not
                                    bring
The flowers of the season to my grave;
There in the April days I will not
                                    have
Upon the granite chips discreetly laid
Wild singing daffodils for orchards
                                    made,
Pale flights of jonquils on a marble
                                    plinth,
The water-white narcissus watching
                                    Spring
With open eye crying the earth's
                                    release;
But more than all if there's a
                                    hyacinth
Filling my darkened channel to the sky,
I ask you then - how shall I rest in
                                    peace
Or be content to die?

122

Spring Flowers

If in the Spring I die you must not bring
The flowers of the season to my grave;
There in the April days I will not have
Upon the granite chips discreetly laid
Wild singing daffodils for orchards made,
Pale flights of jonquils on a marble plinth,
The water -white narcissus, watching Spring
With open eye, crying the earth's release;
But more than all, if there's a hyacinth
Filling my darkened channel to the sky,
I ask you then – how shall I rest in peace
Or be content to die?

Is It Hard To Remember?

Is it hard to remember the dead?
The dead that lived and moved and walked,
The dead that laughed and hoped and talked
And turned to listen to what you said -
Is it hard to remember the dead?

To remember them doing the ordinary things
That every day's awaking brings;
Bound by ordinary mortal fetters:
Drinking tea and writing letters,
Catching cold in the winter rains,
Standing in queues and catching trains,
Drawing blinds on the morning sun,
Being cross and making fun,
Cleaning their teeth and going to bed -
Is it hard to remember the dead?

Do you think of them always hedged about
With the shadow of death that found them out?
Is every word they ever spoke,
And every thought and deed and joke,
Every breath they breathed, every sigh they sighed
Ravished, because of the fact they *died*?

Something was wrong - they had to die,
They never were truly alive as I,
They never were truly known and loved,
Or how could they be so far removed
To a country where I shall never go,
To a land I swear I shall never know?
Give me the meanest life instead!
It is hard to remember the dead.
Is this the way of your reasoning please?
The thoughts you have are they thoughts like these?
I am young and not so wise.

Is it hard to remember the way their eyes
Would be on waking, when you were there,
To watch them suddenly grow aware
And smile a little, and shut again?
Is it hard to remember that all their pain
Was deep and real as the tears you shed?
Is it hard to remember the dead?

Why keep on with the old refrain –
Repeating the question again and again –
Anyway, why do you want to know?
Well, you see, I died, not an hour ago.

Bombay, January 1946.

November

The land gives up its secrets: who'd have known
A pool lay shining in the wood?
Or could have guessed how startling and how good
The line of the hill through the empty trees?
The oaks have come triumphantly into their own.

Through the thinning hedge the naked bank
Brown as peat, bloomed as a grape,
Shows lean of shoulder and proud of flank,
And all the trim of summer's ease
Is lost to find this quiet shape.

The wind is a wind of a thousand groans,
The hill is dark and grey with rain,
But the strength of the land with its lovely bones
Is here for our comfort again.

Autumn Afternoon

How still you stand my sad, grey trees
Stretching cold fingers towards the sky,
Yellow leaves lie in a drifted mound
Or scattered and cold on the hardening ground
Dying, as we shall die.

Death of the year - but a silent death,
Now rain storms and the wild winds cease,
Blue wood smoke drifts from garden fires,
And burning leaves make funeral pyres,
That the year may die - in peace.

London, November 1935.

Puget Sound

I was drowned
In Puget Sound
On a morning of mist
That dipped and kissed
The water's shining face;
The thrusting grace
Of fir and pine -
Black jagged line -
Daggered the opal sky
I was drowned
In Puget Sound
What better way to die?

Tacoma, November 1939.

The Rose

If you had died the rose could turn to stone
Forever fastened in the lighted air;
Not all the world's corrosion could impair
Petals of coral, frozen core of gold,
A fossil in a summer of its own
Finding no climate wherein to grow old.

But since you live and breathe and grow you must
So lives the rose. Pollen blows away,
And hour by hour, nibblings of decay
Consume the petal: stamen rust:
And breadth of June – to winter's measure thinned
Will leave for us a dry thorn in the wind.

The Gate

And when we have passed the gate and known the way,
We'll stand with quiet reflective eyes, and turn and say
One to another:- "Why did we strive
With all our will and energy to stay alive?"

The End Of The Day

We move through the afterglow forward into the twilight,
Hoping, perhaps, to have lighted the lamp in our hand,
For otherwise, surely, we shall find only darkness,
In the night-time land.

The Shock Of Dying

Before I must meet the shock of dying
Let me diffuse the edge that is I,
Spread me out to include the flying
Night wind under the broad night sky.
If I were not persistently me,
But blended out to the shape of things,
Would I not find it easier passing
Into the light where morning sings?
And if my being did not hover
In a pointed singleness,
Living, could I not discover
Death's all-minded consciousness?

Delhi - Jhelum, March 1945

Amid the unceasing round of starts and flurries
My heart is busy at its usual game
The manufacturing of woes and worries
Lest the serene of life should seem too tame

Written early on the morning of Christmas Day 1992 –
her last Christmas

MOLLY DRAKE
The Songs

Happiness

Happiness is like a bird with twenty wings,
Try to catch him as he flies,
Happiness is like a bird that only sings,
When his head is in the skies.

You can try to make him walk beside you,
You can say the door is open wide,
If you grab at him: woe betide you,
I know because I've tried.

Like a butterfly upon an April morning,
Very quickly taking fright,
Happiness is come and gone without a warning,
Jack O' Lantern in the night.

I will follow him across the meadow,
I will follow him across the hill,
And if I can catch him I will try to bring you,
Why yes, Happiness.

If I can catch him I will try to bring you,
All my love, and happiness.

Little Weaver Bird

Little Weaver bird sitting sadly in the tree,
Take my good advice and forget your misery,
Your tears are all in vain and regret can be absurd,
Little Weaver bird get weaving.

The year is going by and the season's getting on,
Don't you think it's time to build yourself a home,
She blinked a brilliant eye I don't even think she heard,
Little Weaver bird get weaving.

Your children will arrive and expect a downy bed,
For everything alive needs a place to lay its head,
She looked at me and sighed but she never said a word,
Little Weaver bird get weaving.

Oh I can sympathise with a heart that is distressed,
But every bird who's wise will build herself a nest,
She looked at me and sighed and a miracle occurred,
The little Weaver bird got weaving.

Cuckoo Time

I wish it were cuckoo time sweet lovely cuckoo time,
Wish it were cuckoo time, the month of May,
Oh that was a cuckoo time,
Sweet crazy cuckoo time,
Morning of all the year, break of day.

But now it's swallow time and swallows in the sky,
Are ready to spread their wings and fly,
And with the swallow time,
The year is on the wing,
Only a memory of spring.

Oh how did it pass me by sweet lovely cuckoo time?
Did I not notice when the year was young?
Can I remember still
That cuckoo time?
Now that the cuckoo song is sung.

Love Isn't A Right

Love isn't a right it's got to be earned,

Love isn't a right, (that's got to be learned),

Maybe you spent your natural life,

Loving husband or loving wife,

Were you loving and was your love returned?

Love's nobody's fool and nobody's slave,

Love won't go to school and learn to behave,

Ride your love on an easy rein,

If love can go it comes back again,

Love will haunt us from cradle to the grave.

Love's a whisper,

Loves a SHOUT,

Love's a flame that could blow out,

Love's all beauty but make it a duty,

And love will lie right down and die.

Love, love is a germ you'll never resist,

Love, love's the eternal Will O' The Wisp,

Follow him through the darkest day,

Love will glimmer and light your way,

Grab at him and he flickers away out of sight.

Love's enchanted,

Don't take it for granted,

For love, isn't a right.

Dream Your Dreams

I don't believe the sun would shine again,
Or that the world would keep on turning,
If it were not for all the dreams of men,
The hoping, the longing, the yearning.

For what the poet said is true enough it seems,
We are the substance and the stuff of dreams.

So dream your dreams and let them keep out the cold,
Dreaming dreams a heart can never grow old,
Give yourself a new mentality,
What's so hot about reality?

Dream your dreams if it's the last thing you do,
Never mind if they don't ever come true,
Something grows from them that's light and gleaming,
The seed of magic lies in all our dreaming.

How Wild The Wind Blows

The acorn carries an oak tree,
Sleeping but for a little while,
Winter lies in the arms of spring,
As a mother carries her child.

And never knows...
How wild the wind blows.

A thought carries a universe,
A seed carries a field of grain,
Love lies in the arms of change,
As a joy carries a pain.

And no-one knows...
How wild the wind blows.

What Can A Song Do To You?

Music from an open window,
Music sudden and fleeting,
Ordinary music in an ordinary street,
Why does your heart stop beating.

What can a song do to you?
Can it waken a memory sleeping,
Can it call back a day,
When your heart fled away,
Into somebody else's keeping.

What can a song do to you?
Can it bring back a Spring in December,
Can it make, with each note,
Such an ache in your throat,
That you find you can still remember.

For the past is a house full of treasure,
And there lies buried deep in the store,
Every smile every tear every pleasure,
And a song is the key to the door.

What can a song do to you?
Can it kindle a flame that was dying,
'Til it burns once again,
With its joy, with its pain,
And your heart's of a sudden crying.

Oh I know, yes I know now I see,
What a song has done to me.

I Remember

We tramped the open moorland in the rainy April weather,
And came upon the little inn that we had found together,
The landlord gave us toast and tea and stopped to share a joke,
And I remember firelight,
I remember firelight,
I remember firelight,
And you remember smoke.

We ran about the meadow grass with all the harebells bending,
And shaking in the summer wind the Summer never ending,
We wandered to the little stream among the river flats,
And I remember willow trees,
I remember willow trees,
I remember willow trees,
And you remember gnats.

We strolled the Spanish market place at ninety in the shade,
With all the fruit and vegetables so temptingly arrayed,
And we can share a memory as every lover must,
And I remember oranges,
I remember oranges,
I remember oranges,
And you remember dust.

The Autumn leaves are tumbling down and winter's almost here,
But through the Spring and Summer time
  we laughed away the year,
And now we can be grateful for the gift of memory,
When I remember having fun,
Two happy hearts that beat as one,
When I had thought that we were we,
But we were you and me.

A Sound

A sound can take you where it will
A sound can make your heart stand still
Like summer rain that drips from leaf to leaf
Can bring alive again an old forgotten grief

A sound can take you by the hand
To wander in an ancient land of long ago
When we were very young
And still so many songs unsung

The web is woven, the net is cast
The spell is made, oh let it last
When time had never brushed his wing
Said his say, had his fling

A sound when someone says your name
All at once a tiny tongue of flame
Oh I cannot speak
I dare not turn around
And yet I know I know I know
It's just a sound.

Ballad

If you can see the strong unwearied starlight,
Riding the mountains of the night astride,
And as you stand alone,
Within the breathing darkness,
I'll be at your side.

If you can look on this unchanging sunlight,
One second fully when the day is new,
And as the burning coin,
Dazzles beneath your eyelids,
I shall look at you.

And if you can run where wind may beat about you,
Out on the hill where shadows race,
Touching grass,
Touching trees,
And the edge of water,
I shall touch your face.

Though all the lands of heaven and earth divides us,
Though distance is a dark unbroken tether,
If you can walk within the same remembered music,
We can walk,
We can walk together.

Woods In May

Always in woods in May there is a feeling
Something too long withheld will soon be plain
Woods in May in sunlight after rain
Hold always a secret on the tip of their tongue
Perhaps if we stand very still very long
We shall hear the sunlight
See the cuckoo's song

Night Is My Friend

Night is my friend,
For when the busy day goes by,
A sad and lonely heart have I,
Night is my friend.

Long days I spend,
And though I go from place to place,
I seek and never find your face,
Night is my friend.

For when the lights are burning low,
And I am on my own,
I close my eyes and then I know,
That I am not alone.

For night in the end,
Will bring to me that peace of mind,
And comfort all true lovers find,
Their dreams can send.

So night,
Sweet lovely night's,
My friend.

Fine Summer Morning

On a fine Summer morning the bird on the wing,
Is singing his heart out as though it were.... Spring,
The whole pretty scene,
Is a patchwork of green,
On a fine summer morning.

On a fine Summer morning the day will be long,
The air full of blossom the tree full of song,
Out of the skylight,
No glimpse of the twilight,
On a fine Summer morning.

There's a new day-a-dawning a new lease of life,
A rose has no thorn a wind no knife,
Who's to remember,
The dark of December?
On a fine Summer morning.

Set Me Free

Chained like a tune in a hurdy,
Chained as the moon is to the tide,
Caught in the web of a destiny,
That I cannot cast aside.

Tossed in a whip of a whirlpool,
Lost like a ship without a chart,
Let me escape from the tyranny of,
This aching breaking heart.

Set me free, don't keep me bound to you,
Set me free, and let me go.

Why should I be wrapped in this sadness,
Trapped in this madness,
Deep as a spell,
Deeper than hell.

Set me free, oh let me break away,
Forget to grieve, for one whole night and day

Forget this thing I crave
That makes a slave of me
If you don't want me bound
Unfetter me
And set me free

Breakfast At Bradenham Woods

It was dark and cold,
It was April cold,
The very beginning of day,
I was just about twelve years old,
Long ago and far away.

But it's one of the things I remember still,
I always have and I always will,
The sun coming up like a dazzling cup,
Just over Salterton Hill.

Then there was...

Breakfast at Bradenham Woods in the years of the morning,
Mornings at seven to borrow what Browning would say,
Heaven could never lay on,
Such a clamour of birdsong,
The larch the primrose, sunlight slanting and gay,

Breakfast at Bradenham Woods and without any warning,
A magic was made that has stayed for the whole of my life,
I could never go back without breaking the spell,
Well then I'll never try,
For breakfast at Bradenham Woods I must keep 'til I die.

Never Pine For The Old Love

There's a moment that I have longed for
We would meet after all these years
I can imagine the thrill of it
For I still think of all our dreams and tears
I see flowers and candlelight
And a tablecloth checked in red
And we sit holding hands
In our own small world
And never a word is said

For we so often pine for the old love
Pine, tender and true
Often pine for the old love
Rather than find the new

Now's the moment that I have dreamed of
Here we are on the fateful day
Hand in hand
Not a word is said
For we haven't got a thing to say
Here we sit in the candlelight
Waiting for the thrill to start
With the red checked tablecloth between us
We're twenty million miles apart

Oh you should never pine for the old love
Pine, tender and true
Never pine for the old love
Go out and find the new

Hey hey hey
But the world keeps turning
Here is something the evening showed
You go away and you grow away
And you travel a separate road
You take a dream just to keep you warm
As milestones pass you by
But you are a different person
And surprisingly so am I

So you should never pine for the old love
Pine, tender and true
Never pine for the old love
Go out and find the new.

Poor Mum

Poor mum, poor mum
After a lifetime of dreaming

Poor mum, poor mum
whatever became of your scheming?

Nothing worked out in the way that you planned
Nothing was quite as you thought

Try very hard not to misunderstand,
Joy as it flies cannot be caught

Poor mum, poor mum
where did you take a wrong turning?

Poor mum, poor mum
pack up that last little yearning

pack it away with the books and the toys
Silent and dumb silent and mum

Go out and grab at your life and forget

you were poor, poor...

...Mum?

Do You Ever Remember?

Do you ever remember?
Now you are so far away
Things that we used to laugh about
Crazy things we'd say
There were so many May times
When every word was a song
There were so many gay times
Before it all went oh so wrong

But time is ever a vagabond
Time was always a thief
Time can steal away happiness
But time can take away grief
So I won't try to remember
For that way leads to regret
No I won't try to remember
What I can never forget

The First Day

This is the first day of the rest of my life
Could be the first day of the best of my life
There could be sunlight, there could be rain
But losing or winning, this is beginning all over again

This is the birthday of a brand new start
Change of direction, change of heart

When I think of today I feel tempted to say
Destiny, do your worst
Of the rest of the days of the rest of my life
It's only the first

Each little day is a world of its own
Each little day is a tomb
Whenever the day has drifted away
It's back to the womb

As I lie alone in the darkness
Waiting the next rebirth
I say for me what could very well be
For everyone else on earth

This is the first day of the rest of my life
Could be the first day of the best of my life
There could be sunlight, there could be rain
But losing or winning, this is beginning all over again

This is the birthday of a brand new start
Change of direction, change of heart

When I think of today I feel tempted to say
Destiny, do your worst
Of the rest of the days of the rest of my life
This is only the first.

Funny Little Tune

Funny little tune
Risen from the ground
Funny thing, but yesterday
You didn't even have a sound -
Funny little tune
Borrowed from the air,
Funny thing, but yesterday
You just weren't there

Tell me, were you born
From the wind and rain?
And will you return
To them once again?
Please, oh please don't you escape,
Aren't you glad to have a shape?
Is that why you found my ear
And got inside my brain?

Funny little tune
I am very proud
That you should have chosen me
And I will sing you very loud;
Funny little tune
Borrowed from the air
Funny thing, but yesterday
You just weren't there.

Some Other Spring

There'll be some other spring
I doubt it not
There'll be some other spring
When this sweet spring
Is quite forgot
Some other blackbird singing from some other hill
Some other dawn beginning will make my heart stand still

There'll be some other name
Some April day
A spark will turn to flame
Some starry night in May
Now that the world seems so bereft of everything
Let me remember there will be some other spring

Laugh Of The Year

I never thought I was glamorous
Nor dreamed I could inspire
Feelings that were amorous
Red-hot flames of desire
But now the door has opened on
A land of milk and honey
It's wonderful, it's marvellous
But Lord! It's terribly funny:

It's the laugh of the year
That you love me true
I could understand if you thought I was grand
As a mother, a sister or brother
But no one ever before
Made me feel so dear,
And although I know it's a thrill
It is still the laugh of the year.

Road To The Stars

Everywhere you go
There's a certain glow
Shining out to comfort and to cheer me
Take me by the hand
To the promised land
Everything seems easy when you're near me

There's a road to the stars
But I don't know the way
We could go to the stars
If you would show the way
All alone on my own I go round and round
But I can't get my feet off the ground.
Yet with you there beside me
The darkness would be light,
With your radiance to guide me
I'd conquer every height
And we might get a sight
Of the brightness of heaven
If you'd show me
The road to the stars

Lullaby

All things are resting,
Each little nestling
Out in the windy dark
On the bough
Folds up his pretty wings,
Hushed are the twitterings –
My little nestling
Bye-byes now.

Each little fledgling
Under the hedgling
Under the darkening sky
Bye-byes now;
Swallow and turtle dove,
Sparrow and starling, -
My little darling
Bye-byes now.

Give Me A Place To Be

by Gabrielle Drake

Chapter taken from the book *Remembered For A While*

by Cally Callomon and Gabrielle Drake

(John Murray 2014)

Rodney Shuttleworth Drake was born in 1908, the only son, and youngest child, of Violet and Ernest Drake. His father, Ernest, was an eminent Harley Street physician, and was able to send his son to Marlborough College – the school he had himself attended.

The original intention was for Rodney to go to university after leaving school, study medicine, and follow in his father's footsteps. However, the family fortunes were badly affected when Ernest Drake suffered a heart attack and had to give up his lucrative London practice and retire to the country. Rodney had to leave Marlborough, and there was now no question of him going to university.

Thanks to the kind offices of 'a wealthy relation', Rodney secured an apprenticeship with the London and North Eastern Railway, and trained at their depots in Darlington and York, whilst studying for his engineering degree at night school.

If this change of plan dismayed Rodney, he certainly never showed it. Indeed, he might even have secretly welcomed it, for he seemed to be a born engineer, and always looked back on his time in the North-East with considerable affection.

However, his training accomplished, he decided that a future with the railways was not for him; so in 1930, ripe for adventure, he applied for, and got, a job as an Engineer Assistant with the Bombay Burmah Trading Corporation (BBTC) – an established British company in the Far East, with extensive interests in the teak industry.

Rodney was posted to Burma (now Myanmar). This must have been the first time he had been out of Europe – maybe even out of England, bearing in mind the restricted travel conditions of his time. But, from the moment he set foot on board the SS *Gloucestershire*, bound for Rangoon (Yangon), he seems to have been in his element. His first letter home to his parents is an enthusiastic, day-by-day chronicle of his first week at sea – by the end of which he had already been commandeered by the Captain to organise a gala day of games, had formed a committee to do this, and been, as he puts it,

'attacked by a crowd of energetic females who complained that there were not enough events for the women. I asked the leader of this deputation to become a member of the committee (a stroke of tactical genius on my part!) . . .[and] we got the games drawn up by midnight.'

All the elements that were key to his success in life are apparent in this little incident: leadership, tact, an ability to delegate, and a self-deprecating irony, all packaged in a charm that made it easy for these talents to be recognised by his superiors.

These included his boss at the BBTC in Rangoon. Rodney described their first meeting thus:

'I was introduced to one Macnamara – an enormous great genial fellow who, I have since learned, is an important man to keep on the right side of. It appears that he can be extraordinarily nice when he likes (and vice versa!) .

171

. . we were soon involved in a long discussion on a series of calculations he had been making in connection with a steam plant – I found myself to be in complete disagreement with several of his solutions and informed him of the fact. However, we got on very well.'

Indeed they did, for Rodney advanced speedily in the company, and was soon given the responsibility of constructing a large new sawmill in Rangoon, which he then operated as Mill Manager. Many years later, it would be Macnamara who would offer him the managerial job that brought him back to England.

But for now, Rodney threw himself into his new life, declaring to his parents, 'I think I am going to like the job enormously, and the life as well.'

'The life', for the young men who had come out East to help run either the British Administration or British industrial enterprises, consisted of playing as hard as they worked: swimming, golf – played very early in the morning to escape the heat – tennis, squash, rowing, as well as expeditions into the jungle to shoot snipe, were all interspersed with a hard day's work at the office. And in the evenings there were dances, dinners in the Club – the great hub of social life – and amateur plays and concerts: for 'Out East' there was no choice but to provide your own entertainment. Rodney was a popular performer: he played the piano well enough to entertain his friends after dinner (sometimes with his own compositions: he once wrote an operetta based on life on board a ship bound for the East), and sang in a fine bass voice – a fact attested to by this review of the Boat Club Concert, lovingly kept by his mother:

'Mr R.S. Drake's 'Droop Not Young Lover' brought the house down. Before he opened his mouth, there was applause, but this is due to Mr Drake's popularity. Not even the singer took the song seriously. I felt that Mr Drake himself was doing his best not to laugh. But in spite of this, he sang extremely well . . . The audience begged for more . . .'

The year 1933 was to prove momentous for Rodney – not that he realised it at the time. He would have known the Deputy Commissioner, one Idwal Lloyd, and his formidable wife Georgie; and also known their eldest daughter, Gwladys, a noted beauty who had come out to Burma with her parents shortly before he had. In December of that year, the Lloyds returned from leave, bringing with them their second daughter, Molly, then aged eighteen.

Molly Lloyd was born in 1915 in Rangoon. Her father, Idwal, was a serving officer in the elite Indian Civil Service, and had been posted to Burma – then a province of India. She was christened Mary, but Molly seemed a much more appropriate name for the little girl with flaming red hair – and Molly she remained for the rest of her life.

In those days, the Far East was not considered to be a healthy environment for children; so, at the age of three, Molly had been taken back to England. There, she, and her two sisters – elder sister Gwladys, and younger sister Nancy – were brought up in the happy household of the Dunns. Aunt Helen and Uncle Willie, despite straitened circumstances, seem to have had a gift for creating happiness and giving their extended family of servicemen's children a haven in which to flourish. What could have been a time of disastrous unhappiness therefore turned out to be one of joyous development, where the bond between Molly and her younger sister Nancy was irrevocably forged. It would last their entire lives.

All three girls were eventually sent to boarding school. Molly always professed to having hated school, although she managed to scrape through her School Certificate. Having done so, she was, to her joy, allowed to leave school and return with her parents to Burma.

Her diary for the year 1933 shows great exuberance and *joie de vivre*; and her record of the sea journey out East curiously mirrors Rodney's description to his parents of his own voyage two years earlier. But, unlike Rodney, Molly was desperately shy. She felt herself to be gauche and awkward – and feared letting down her glamorous elder sister Gwladys, who had already cut a swathe through Rangoon society. However, with the casting aside of school uniform, ugly glasses, and straight hair (her first perm must have been a great joy to her), a butterfly emerged from the chrysalis, and, despite her fears, Molly seems to have had little difficulty finding her place in the carefree whirl of colonial life in those pre-war years in Burma.

Molly met Rodney Drake at one of the first parties she went to in Rangoon – unsurprisingly, since he was a sought-after guest at most social events. It was not love at first sight. But his easy wit and life-long ability to set people at their ease must have been a great comfort to the shy young Molly. However, it would be some time before either of them recognised that they had found a partner for life. They eventually married in 1937: it was to be a marriage that endured, vibrantly, for fifty-one years, until Rodney's death in 1988.

The early years of their marriage were set against increasing political unrest. Burma was granted separate colonial status in 1937, with much of the governing power devolving to the indigenous people. However, calls for total independence became ever louder, and strikes were frequent. Nevertheless, life for the colonials seems to have continued to be relatively carefree and easy. And despite the storm clouds that were gathering over Europe, when letters from 'Home' took several weeks to arrive, it was difficult to grasp of the immediacy of any situation. If the 'Phoney War' in England was a time of unnatural calm, so much the more was it Out East.

The grim reality of the Second World War finally came to Burma in 1942 with the Japanese invasion. Hasty plans were made for the evacuation of the British women, and Molly and her sister Nancy – now married to Rodney's close friend in Burma, Chris McDowall – joined the great trek out of Burma into India. For the most part, this turned into a mad scramble, with evacuees suffering appalling hardship and loss of life. But Molly and Nancy had the good fortune to be part of a comparatively well-organised march. Nevertheless, it was gruelling: the terrain was difficult, and the threat constant, and underlying everything was a constant anguish as to the fate of their husbands, who were in the thick of the fighting in Burma.

If Molly's retreat out of Burma was difficult, Rodney's was worse. He had already enlisted in the Burma Defence Force, but now, with the fall of Rangoon, he joined the Artisan Works company, where his engineering skills were used to lay charges for the demolition of bridges, which must, in itself, have been depressing for a construction engineer.

The Allied retreat out of Burma was a desperate and disorganised affair and Rodney was in the thick of it. Starving, sick and wounded refugees clogged the primitive roads leading to India, and harassment by the Japanese, who had an intimate knowledge of the jungle terrain, was constant and effective. At Shwegin, Rodney had the unenviable job of Embarkation Officer. Here General Alexander's Burma Corps had to be ferried across the Chindwin River on ramshackle ferries, and under unceasing enemy attack. Eventually the Corps – depleted and with virtually no equipment – reached India, just as the monsoon broke. The demoralised men found their miseries added to when they were forced to camp in the open under torrential rain. Rodney, among many others, fell victim to dysentery. He was eventually granted sick leave, and was able to join Molly.

By now, Molly and Nancy had taken refuge with their aunt and uncle, Alan and Mary Lloyd, in Delhi, seat of the British Administration in India. Alan Lloyd, like his brother Idwal, was a member of the ICS, and part of the government – a government that seemed almost unaware of the war being fought on its borders. Life for the two sisters must now have taken on a surreal similarity to life in Burma before the war. Not least since their Aunt Mary, though delightful and loving, was as formidable a member of the British Raj as ever their mother had been, and made it quite clear that the girls must not 'let the side down'. Stiff upper lips were the order of the day. The sisters took comfort from each other; and since both were musical it was perhaps inevitable, at a time when party pieces were expected, that they should form a duet, singing together, unaccompanied, in close harmony. So successful were they that they were asked to perform on All India Radio. Nancy, whose

1955, (L-R) Rodney, Gabrielle and Nick Drake,
Chris McDowall, Molly Drake and her sister
Nancy McDowall

knowledge of music was more academic than her sister's, would arrange
popular songs of the era for them to perform. For Molly, though, music was a
private joy. As was her poetry. All her life, both provided a retreat and a place
from which to draw inner strength. And though she was happy to play and
sing her songs to friends and family, their composing was always an intensely
private affair, and she would sit for hours alone at a piano, working out words
and music. Her poetry, she would read to Nancy.

When Rodney eventually reached Delhi, riddled with dysentery, Molly's
joy must have been laced with alarm. He arrived with only the ragged clothes
he stood up in (he had already been refused entry into the British Club,
because he was not wearing a dinner jacket!), and though six feet tall weighed
no more than seven stone. His recovery was long and slow – particularly as
dysentery developed into hepatitis.

By the time Rodney was declared fit, the Japanese occupation of Burma
had severed India's vitally needed supply of teak. So it was that Rodney

found himself seconded out of the army, and commissioned by the Indian government to build a sawmill at the foot of the Himalaya mountains. This meant that he and Molly could live together again in the little hill station of Jhelum – provided he could find suitable accommodation. The mill duly arrived in packing cases from America and, once built, Rodney, ever ingenious, constructed a house for himself and Molly out of the redundant packing cases. 'Packing Case Villa' saw the birth of their first child, Gabrielle.

Rodney had given an undertaking to the BBTC that, as soon as the war ended, he would return to Burma. And immediately after the Japanese surrender in 1945, this is what he did, taking charge of the efforts to restore his firm's fortunes there. But much more than this, he had become deeply involved in the politics of country. He had grown to love Burma, and grieved at the devastation war had wrought upon a once wealthy country, rich in rice and oil and teak. Now devastated by the scorched-earth policies of both the British and the Japanese, the country was in chaos. Rodney had spent many hours deliberating on a solution for Burma, and wrote a long paper detailing his ideas. The plan that he set out for independence was coherent, radical, and took into account all he had learned of the Burmese people. He always believed that independence for the country was both essential and inevitable. But he also believed that Britain had a moral responsibility to ensure that this happened gradually, and with the requisite amount of education and support from the British government. Although well received by the authorities – and this included Sir Stafford Cripps, at the time a member of the War Cabinet – it was, in the end, ignored. Nevertheless, when the post-war Administration was set up in Rangoon, Rodney was one of only four European members of the House of Representatives. All his tact and diplomatic skills were needed during this highly charged time of political instability.

No doubt to Rodney's dismay, three brief years later, in January 1948, Burma was granted full independence. Much of the turmoil he had predicted would follow such a precipitate event came to pass; and his tract 'Chaos in Burma' remains a fine analysis of the troubles that ensued.

However, the Drakes now also had personal matters on their minds. For five months later, in June, their second child – Nicholas Rodney – was born in Rangoon: possibly in the same hospital where Molly had herself been born. With the political situation becoming ever more volatile in the wake of independence, it must have been something of a relief when, in 1949, the BBTC offered Rodney promotion, sending him to their head offices in Bombay, where he became a director and joint chairman.

But not for long. In 1950, Rodney's erstwhile boss, that 'great genial fellow' Macnamara, wrote to him from England, offering him a job as managing director of a small Birmingham-based firm, the Wolseley Sheep Shearing Company. To leave India would be a wrench for the whole family – Rodney and Molly loved the life Out East. On the other hand, they knew they would soon be faced with the problem of their children's education, which would have to take place in England in a few years, and this would inevitably lead to the family being split up. Much as she had enjoyed her childhood with the Dunns, Molly didn't want the same fate for her children, and she and Rodney found the thought of separation from each other, if she accompanied the children back to England, intolerable. So with considerable sorrow, the Drakes packed up, lock, stock and barrel, and trundled back home, taking with them the children's Karen nanny, Rosie PawTun.

In fact, Nanny – as Rosie was always known (having been nanny in England to other retired colonial families) – knew more about 'Home' – an austere post-war England – than either Molly or Rodney did themselves. She it was who guided Molly through the complexities of post-war rationing, and helped her set up a household without servants, something Molly had never known before in her married life.-

The family moved to the leafy county of Warwickshire: Shakespeare's county. Rodney bought his wife a house which, at the time, he could ill afford, but which Molly had fallen in love with. Far Leys was spacious and well-proportioned, and looked out over an expansive garden to the glorious Warwickshire countryside beyond. Molly made it both elegant and comfortable; and the sitting room, with its central feature of their grand piano, transported back from Bombay, became a hub of legendary social events – often music-based, for both Rodney and Molly were proficient piano players. In an age when television was still a rarity, this would not have been so uncommon. What was, perhaps, less usual, was the fact that many snippets of these parties were recorded: For Rodney, ever intrigued by new inventions, had brought home one day a large trunk-like contraption that turned out to be an early reel-to-reel tape-recording machine. Such a novelty was inevitably brought out at parties, and people delighted at the new phenomenon of being able to hear recordings of their own voices. More importantly, as it turned out, Rodney was able to persuade Molly to record her own songs. Understanding, as he always did, the private nature of her creative work, he would set up the machine, and leave her to record her songs on her own. For the sitting room was also Molly's retreat, where, usually in the afternoons, she would sit at the piano, or at her desk, composing, or writing her poetry.

Meanwhile, Rodney rose rapidly in the Birmingham business world, gradually transforming the Wolseley Sheep Shearing Company into what would eventually become a global enterprise. Today, Wolseley plc is the world's largest trade distributor of plumbing and heating products; it was set on that track by Rodney, who developed the small agricultural firm he came to Birmingham to manage into a network of flourishing businesses. He was elected to the Council of the Birmingham Chamber of Commerce, and was president-elect, when history cruelly repeated itself. In 1964, like his father before him, he had a heart attack, and was forced to resign.

The Drakes sent both their children to the schools they had themselves attended. The fact that neither child followed a conventional career path after school worried them not one whit – they almost seemed to feel that their children were pursuing a destiny which was a natural follow-on from their own lives, in which music, drama and literature had featured so significantly in their leisure hours.

Both parents delighted in their son's songwriting ability, though they were not in the least surprised by it; and both were immensely proud of Nick's albums. And later, both faced the ordeal of their son's depressive illness – during the last years of which he spent the majority of his time at home – with baffled fortitude, with extraordinary patience, and with a never-ceasing desire to understand – Rodney with his keen analytic intelligence, Molly with her intuition. From her poetry, one realises that she must have understood much of what her son was going through – yet she was powerless to help him.

Nick's death on a bleak November morning in 1974 was the greatest tragedy of Molly's and Rodney's lives. No one can know the toll it took on them both. Outwardly they recovered, drawing strength, once again, from each other, as well as, over the following years, from any recognition given to their son's music – including the small stream of his fans that came to visit Far Leys from all over the world. Alas, neither of them lived to see the full extent of their son's burgeoning fame.

Rodney died in 1988. His obituary states:

Rodney Drake combined, to a most unusual degree, exceptional skill in all aspects of mechanical engineering with a high order of administrative ability and financial acumen. Intellectually gifted, his fertile brain was a constant source of innovative ideas, the acceptance of which he would seek to achieve by gentle persuasion rather than coercion. He was a thoughtful, sympathetic and wise counsellor to those with personal problems, but above all he was a man of sparkling humour, and laughter was never far away when he was in the room. Truly a man for all seasons, he earned the respect affection and admiration of all with whom he came into contact.

Molly lived on until 1993. She earned no obituary – which was perhaps fitting for such an essentially reclusive person. What would she have made of the fact that strangers across the world are now listening to her own songs and reading her poetry? That both have achieved critical acclaim in America and in Britain? That she has been the subject of a radio programme and a live concert?

For someone who once scribbled her 'Epitaph' in pencil in her poetry book –

> Here lies one who was felled at a touch
> Who purposing many a many thing
> Almost did so much and so much
> And never quite did anything.

– might she not perhaps have said, to quote another line from one of her songs, 'It's the laugh of the year'?

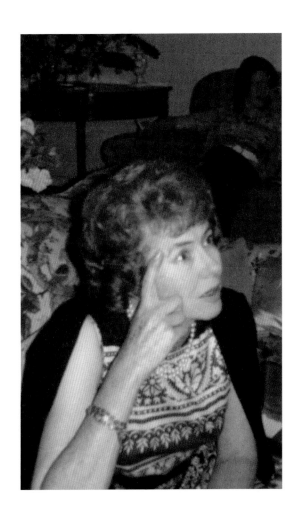

Dream Your Dreams

Dream your dreams and let them keep out the cold

Dream - - - ing dreams a heart can nev-er grow old

Give your-self a new men-tal - - - i - - - ty.

whats so hot a-bout re - al - - - - ty?

Impervious. M & Cº

Dream your dreams if it's the last thing you do.

Nev — er mind if they don't ev-er come true.

Some — thing grows from them that's light and gleam — ing, the

seed of mag-ic lies in all our dream — — ing.

Impervious. M & Co

189

On Monkey Island with children

All poems were written by Molly Drake and remain in copyright to Bryter Music.

All songs were written by Molly Drake except for the lyrics to 'Oh To Be In England' which is a poem by Robert Browning (1812 – 1889) set to music by Molly Drake, and the lyrics to The Oak And The Ash (also known as North Country Maid) which is a traditional song. The arrangement for this was by Molly's sister Nancy McDowall.

All songs were originally recorded by Rodney Drake at Far Leys, Tanworth In Arden on a variety of home recorders. These were digitally transferred and produced by John Wood. All tracks were mastered by Simon Heyworth at Super Audio Mastering, Chagford, England.

The recordings were lifted from various magnetic reel-to-reel tapes that were set to run at an economical slow speed designed mainly for home listening, they were never intended for commercial release. The sound quality found in these transcriptions reflects this and little has been done to alter their original condition.

All songs are published by Domino Publishing

Book design and packaging is by Cally (antar.cc) aided by Nik Rose
Book production: John Garrad at Akcent Media

Grateful thanks go to all those credited above as well as John Garrad, Kieran Jay, Paul Lamden, Adrian McNally, John Murray Publishing, Shane O'Neill, David and Dan at Squirrel Thing, David Suff, The Unthanks.

This edition produced by Gabrielle Drake and Cally Callomon

CD Number One

1. Happiness
2. Little Weaver Bird
3. Cuckoo Time
4. Love Isn't A Right
5. Dream Your Dreams
6. How Wild The Wind Blows
7. What Can A Song Do To You
8. I Remember
9. A Sound
10. Ballad
11. Woods In May
12. Night Is My Friend
13. Fine Summer Morning
14. Set Me Free
15. Breakfast At Braddenham Woods
16. Never Pine For The Old Love
17. Poor Mum
18. Do You Ever Remember?
19. The First Day

CD Number Two

1. Funny Little Tune
2. Some Other Spring
3. The Laugh Of The Year
4. The Road To The Stars
5. Oh To Be In England
6. Lullaby
7. The Oak And The Ash

CD Number One previously released as a private pressing on Bryter Music in 2011

All songs on CD Number two previously unreleased

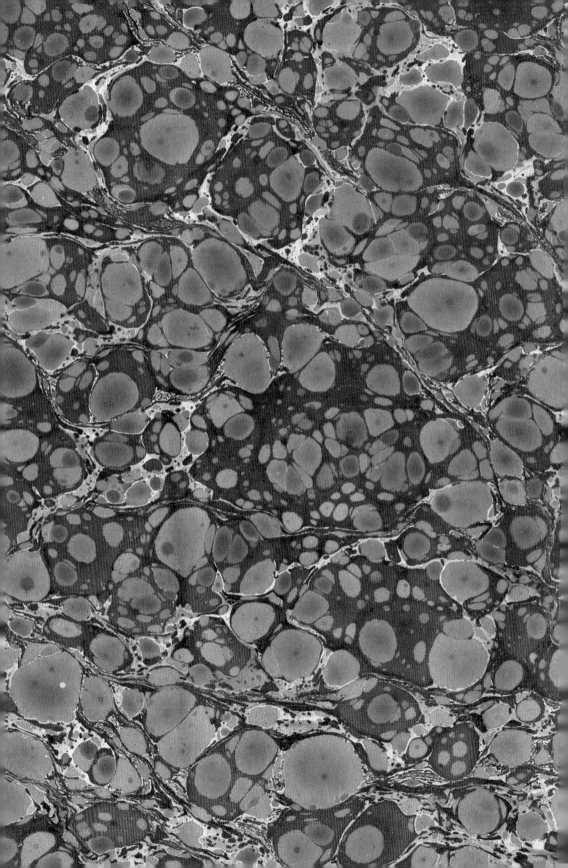